Contents

3 | Letter from the Co-Authors

4 | One Answer to Recidivism - Technology

5 | Marketing is 85% of Your Business

6-11 | Social Media to Sustain Your Business
  | Facebook
  | Twitter
  | Instagram
  | LinkedIn
  | YouTube

12 | Email Marketing

13 | To Blog or Not to Blog

14-15 | How To Write a Book in Less Than 90 Days

16-17 | How to Market a Book for Free

18-19 | Art of the 30 Second Pitch

20-21 | How to Speak for a Living

22-23 | Notes

Letter from the Co-Authors

To anyone that has made the decision to read this book, not just the formerly incarcerated or those that are employment challenged, anyone that had just an ounce of curiosity to see what this is all about…we thank you.

Change does not always come how we want it or when we want it. It doesn't always come sweet with a cherry on top nor does it come quietly. The movement to stop mass incarceration has become quite a loud movement, so we decided to move in the direction that is not being heard so much. We want to help people re-enter society, get their lives back on track, pay their bills so they can support their children and not use the system as a revolving door.

Our company, Dawah International, LLC has been helping inmates from the inside and outside for more than 10 years. Information is key. Knowledge on how to do many things is imperative for returning citizens. Actually re-entering society from prison is met with so many challenges that this book, Jobs For Felons: What Entrepreneurs Need to Know is the follow up to the ever resourceful, *Jobs For Felons: From Inmates to Entrepreneurs*, is two solid educational sources in the Future Entrepreneur Network.

Volume II dives into information on how to sustain a business, Everyone has ideas and wants to start something. Numerous businesses start but many don't sustain. It takes three years to build. Marketing is a large part of building. This book covers all aspects of marketing from social media to email marketing. It's more than a book. It's a resource. Read it once. Read it twice. Read it as many times as needed to understand. And don't forget to take notes!

Jenny & Rufus Triplett
Co Owners of Dawah International, LLC
www.dawahinc.com

One Answer to Recidivism - Technology

"I could not imagine being incarcerated for 5, 10, 15 or even 20 years then being released into a technologically advanced society with no skills"

E ducational opportunities are limited in the prison industrial complex. Some institutions have eliminated courses for higher learning and some have discontinued the privilege of having those courses through correspondence. The rationale of incarcerating an individual with an 8th grade education plus or minus a couple of years, in the new millennium and age of technology, without the benefit of bettering themselves, is a formula for recidivism.

Prisonworld Magazine, a unique prison publication which was targeted to inmates and their families, and no longer in print, brought information to the society that resides behind the wall. Rufus and Jenny Triplett, co-Editors-in-Chief of Prisonworld Magazine, have remained steadfast helping those who are freedom challenged stay abreast of the free world and the challenges they may face upon re-entry.

Jenny Triplett says "there needs to be a class where inmates can enroll to learn technology. We are living in a world where almost no jobs can be worked without basic technology skills. Inmates are being left behind with this wave of growth. Prisoners are becoming more and more like warehouse inventory and the mission of rehabilitation has been lost. Modern technology has to be a part of the plan."

Words with Friends, a very popular Scrabble like application played on a computer or internet connected hand held device, is a model for teaching communication and building one's vocabulary. The structure of the two player game is designed in the spirit of friendly competition. It is a skill that inmates can use to bolster their lacking mental and physical fulfillment as well as become technology social. "

"I am a techie and a gadget person. It's a sign of the times. Technology is used in just about all aspects of my life. I could not imagine being incarcerated for 5, 10, 15 or even 20 years then being released into a technologically advanced society with no skills. I would be devastated and maybe even a little defeated." says Rufus Triplett, Jr.

Federal inmates as well as a few state inmates have access to email through the Corrlinks/Trulincs system. Another email system which is used exclusively for state inmates is JPay. Between these two systems, an application such as Words with Friends could be implemented. This is a forward thinking school of thought but if something does not happen soon, the prisons system will be even more bassakwards than they are reportedly to be.

Jobs For Felons II: What Entrepreneurs Need To Know

Marketing is 85% of Your Business

Digital marketing is one of the effective ways of marketing a product and services over the world by web through Digital marketing technology. It has become essential in today's time and in future because it helps to increase rapidly and allow to win the marketing war amongst competitors. Therefore these are few basic parts of digital marketing you need to follow:

I. Content marketing:

Content is king, and it will always be. There are different types of content like writing blog, creating post, creating videos, photos on social media & sharing it on other online platforms for different motives like brand awareness, lead generation, growth of traffic, increasing customers is mainly called content marketing.

II. Search engine marketing:

Search engine marketing which includes improving SEO and get found higher on the natural search engine. Even advertising on search engine can drive lots of sales over the night.

III. Email marketing:

Email marketing is one of the powerful way to connect your existing customer continuously. It is use for acquiring, engaging, and retaining, customers to help your business thrive.

IV. Social media:

Social media is one of the biggest pieces of the online marketing puzzle today which is going to include Facebook, Twitter, Instagram, Pinterest, LinkedIn and even online shopping sites. Social Media provides a platform for direct communication between your customer's prospects and employees.

V. Mobile marketing:

Mobile marketing is the marketing that occurs over a mobile device, targeted for mobile users. It leverages mobile devices to communicate and engage with customers at any point, to drive brand value and demand for your product or services

Jobs For Felons II: What Entrepreneurs Need To Know

Social Media to Sustain Your Business

	Who is your audience?	How can you reach them?	What are your goals?

CHOOSING THE RIGHT SOCIAL MEDIA PLATFORM FOR YOUR BUSINESS

	Facebook	Twitter	Pinterest	YouTube	LinkedIn	Instagram	Google+
DEMOGRAPHICS	1.3+ Billion users / Ages 25-54 / 60% Female	600 Million users / Ages 18-29	70 Million users / Ages 18-35 / 80% Female	1 Billion users / All ages	600 Million users / Ages 30-49	200 Million users / Ages 18-29	200 Million users / Ages 25-34 / 67% Male
PURPOSE	Building Relationships	News & Articles; Conversation	"Scrapbooking"	Search "How To"	News & Articles; Conversation	Building Relationships; Conversation	News & Articles
BEST FOR	Building Brand Loyalty	Public Relations	Lead Generation; Clothing, Art & Food Businesses	Brand Awareness; Service industry	Business Development; B2B Businesses	Lead Generation; Retail, Art, Food, Entertainment, & Beauty Businesses	SEO; Tech/Design Businesses
DOWNSIDE	Limited Reach	140 characters or less	Images only; Very specific demographic	Resource intensive	Limited interactions	Images only	Not as widely used

CLICK TO ENLARGE

Over the next five pages we will break down social media and how you should be using it for your business. Facebook, Twitter, Instagram, Linkedin & Youtube can keep daily funds streaming into your business if you use them correctly. That may or may not mean not posting prison pictures. If it's a part of your story, people respect that. If it's what you're using as your crutch, that's not going to work. Check out the next pages to see how you can use social media productively and join the ever growing tool for business.

SOCIAL MEDIA 101
A 3 PART WORKSHOP TO HELP YOU
LEARN HOW TO GET PAID $$$
FROM SOCIAL MEDIA

Rufus and Jenny Triplett
A Mashable Social Media Power Couple

(c) 2015 Dawah International, LLC
www.rufusandjennytriplett.com
678-389-2646

SPOTLIGHT

Social Media 101
This 3 part workshop can help the most basic user of social media learn the ins and outs of how to maneuver in this ever changing conglomerate of apps. www.survivingbusinesstips.com

FACEBOOK

Let's start with the tools of social media. Facebook is the biggest of them all. Whether you like it or don't like it, Facebook is winning the social media game in helping people get jobs, reconnect with family, promote products and services and just overall being social. If you're not on Facebook there should be a really good excuse as to why.

The first thing you should do after creating a profile is to make sure you connect with people that are beneficial to you. If you have been in prison a long time and Facebook is new to you, maybe reconnecting with your old buddies might not be a good idea. They will find you eventually but if you are serious about your business, that should not be the first place to start.

Learn the Platform. Anything worth doing is worth doing well. Don't just think it's about creating your profile and posting pics. Learn all of the ins and outs of the platform so that you can be knowledgeable of how to grow your exposure. Yes, it is a free social media tool, but it must be used to its maximum to benefit you in the long run.

Once you have created a brand, post in a way that represents your brand. Alot of brands today are lifestyle brands. One that comes to mind easily is the Kardashians. They are a lifestyle that brand and everything about their lifestyle gets on social media. They have leveraged that lifestyle in order to run successful businesses. Not saying you have to be a Kardashian but it is just an example of what a lifestyle brand is and how it's done successfully. On the flipside of that, the Braxtons are one as well. That's Toni Braxton and her sisters.

Don't get caught in the trap of distraction. Social media can be a huge distraction and a window to the procrastination of your goals. You can find yourself scrolling all day while looking at pics and videos and in turn not getting anything done. Be sure to put your priorities first and limit your screen time so that you can actually get something accomplished daily.

Via Wikipedia

Facebook, Inc. is an American online social media and social networking service company based in Menlo Park, California. Its website was launched on February 4, 2004, Mark Zuckerberg, along with fellow Harvard College students and roommates Eduardo Saverin, Andrew McCollum, Dustin Moskovitz and Chris Hughes.

The founders initially limited the website's membership to Harvard students. Later they expanded it to higher education institutions in the Boston area, the Ivy League schools, and Stanford University. Facebook gradually added support for students at various other universities, and eventually to high school students. Since 2006, anyone who claims to be at least 13 years old has been allowed to become a registered user of Facebook, though variations exist in this requirement, depending on local laws. The name comes from the face book directories often given to American university students. Facebook held its initial public offering (IPO) in February 2012, valuing the company at $104 billion, the largest valuation to date for a newly listed public company. It began selling stock to the public three months later. Facebook makes most of its revenue from advertisements that appear onscreen.

Great Pages to Follow on Facebook:

Lisa Nichols

Daymond John

Brendon Burchard

Side Hustle Pro

Inc Magazine

TWITTER

If you have parents like ours you could hear them saying, what in the world is a Twitter? What you mean you tweetin? The social media technology boom came into full blown storm at the start of the 2010's. Anything could be seen, heard or reported via these live streaming tools that has everyone buzzing. To get the best buzz in real time, you need to be on twitter.

Twitter is great for news and media but it's also great to connect with your customer. You can get real time live feedback from someone that has purchased your product or someone that is interested in your product. It directly connects you with the consumer and it can make you or break you. Where reviews are of the utmost importance, so it positive feedback.

Social media competes with the likes of the city of New York where it never sleeps. As a brand or business, you may not be up in the midnight hour answering and responding to negative feedback. But if you leave it and not respond, it leaves all of those reading it to think that you do not care about your customers. Be sure to respond to all comments and criticisms in a timely manner and remember that others are watching.

A few tips on posting to Twitter. Even when you think no one is seeing it or responding to it, keep posting. Remember that you're a brand and not just someone off the block so think about what you post. Don't always post something that is selling. Post something that shows your personality. Don't get into Twitter beefs with other people. Let people speak their minds, as some will be disrespectful, but think about how that will effect you in the long run. If you need to use it, the block feature is available.

If you are living your dream of being self employed, don't forget to have fun. Don't forget why you started. Don't get all flustered and frustrated when your dream doesn't produce sometimes. Put it into the universe and you never know who may see it or read it.

Follow us on Twitter

Here are some engaging and enlightening people you should follow on Twitter:

@BusinessInsider

@KimGarst

@Mashable

@FastCompany

@Medium

Via wikipedia

Twitter, Inc. (/ˈtwɪtər/) is an American online news and social networking service on which users post and interact with messages known as "tweets". Tweets were originally restricted to 140 characters, but on November 7, 2017, this limit was doubled for all languages except Chinese, Japanese, and Korean.[12] Registered users can post, like, and retweet tweets, but unregistered users can only read them. Users access Twitter through its website interface, through Short Message Service (SMS) or its mobile-device application software ("app").[13] Twitter, Inc. is based in San Francisco, California, and has more than 25 offices around the world.[14] Twitter was created in March 2006 by Jack Dorsey, Noah Glass, Biz Stone, and Evan Williams and launched in July of that year. The service rapidly gained worldwide popularity. In 2012, more than 100 million users posted 340 million tweets a day,[15] and the service handled an average of 1.6 billion search queries per day.[16][17][18] In 2013, it was one of the ten most-visited websites and has been described as "the SMS of the Internet".[19][20] As of 2016, Twitter had more than 319 million monthly active users.[9] Since 2015, and continuing into 2016 and future years, Twitter has also been the home of debates, and news covering Politics of the United States, especially during the 2016 U.S. presidential election, Brett Kavanaugh Supreme Court Nomination, and 2018 United States Midterms, with Twitter proved to be the largest source of breaking news on the day of the 2016 election, with 40 million election-related tweets sent by 10:00 p.m. (Eastern Time) that day.[21]

Jobs For Felons II: What Entrepreneurs Need To Know

INSTAGRAM

Via Wikipedia

Instagram (also known as **IG**[9]) is a photo and video-sharing social networking service owned by Facebook, Inc. It was created by Kevin Systrom and Mike Krieger, and launched in October 2010 exclusively on iOS. A version for Android devices was released a year and 6 months later, in April 2012, followed by a feature-limited website interface in November 2012, and apps for Windows 10 Mobile and Windows 10 in April 2016 and October 2016 respectively.

The app allows users to upload photos and videos to the service, which can be edited with various filters, and organized with tags and location information. An account's posts can be shared publicly or with pre-approved followers. Users can browse other users' content by tags and locations, and view trending content. Users can "like" photos, and follow other users to add their content to a feed.

The service was originally distinguished by only allowing content to be framed in a square (1:1) aspect ratio, but these restrictions were eased in 2015. The service also added messaging features, the ability to include multiple images or videos in a single post, as well as "Stories"—similar to its main competitor Snapchat—which allows users to post photos and videos to a sequential feed, with each post accessible by others for 24 hours each.

After its launch in 2010, Instagram rapidly gained popularity, with one million registered users in two months, 10 million in a year, and 800 million as of September 2017. In April 2012, Facebook acquired the service for approximately US$1 billion in cash and stock. As of October 2015, over 40 billion photos had been uploaded to the service. Although praised for its influence, Instagram has been the subject of criticism, most notably for policy and interface changes, allegations of censorship, and illegal or improper content uploaded by users.

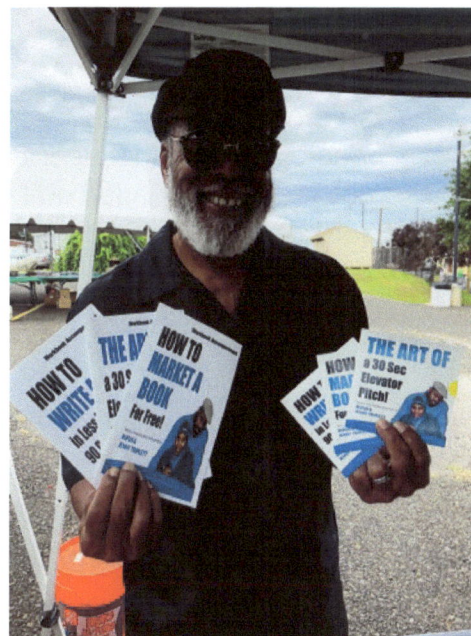

Follow us on Instagram

Use Instagram to showcase cool pics and videos and tell a story about your business, product or service with microblogging. The ABC (S) of business is to Always Be Selling but you don't have to do that on Instagram if you tell stories. You can become very creative with how you showcase your brand.

Interesting people you should follow on Instagram

@RealDLHughley
@TheSharkDaymondJohn
@KendallFicklin
@MrJayMorrison
@ShakaSenghor

9

LINKEDIN

Via Wikipedia

LinkedIn (/lɪŋktˈɪn/) is a business and employment-oriented service that operates via websites and mobile apps. Founded on December 28, 2002,[4] and launched on May 5, 2003,[5] it is mainly used for professional networking, including employers posting jobs and job seekers posting their CVs. As of 2015, most of the company's revenue came from selling access to information about its members to recruiters and sales professionals.[6]

As of October 2018, LinkedIn had 590 million registered members in 200 countries, out of which more than 250 million active users.[3] LinkedIn allows members (both workers and employers) to create profiles and "connections" to each other in an online social network which may represent real-world professional relationships.

Members can invite anyone (whether an existing member or not) to become a connection.[7] The "gated-access approach" (where contact with any professional requires either an existing relationship or an introduction through a contact of theirs) is intended to build trust among the service's members. Since December 2016 it has been a wholly owned subsidiary of Microsoft. LinkedIn participated in the EU's International Safe Harbor Privacy Principles.[8]

If you are looking for a job, LinkedIn is a great tool and resource. You should tighten up your resume and drop it like it's hot on a profile that is complete and telling. LinkedIn is also for networking. You don't have to have or be looking for a conventional 9 to 5 in order to have a profile. Numerous entrepreneurs use the platform to connect with others and build relationships for future business.

Volunteerism is something that you would place on LinkedIn

People you should connect with on LinkedIn:

Carlos Gil

George Fraser

Guy Kawasaki

Richard Branson

Jeff Weiner

YOUTUBE

Via Wikipedia

YouTube, LLC is an American video-sharing website headquartered in San Bruno, California. Three former PayPal employees—Chad Hurley, Steve Chen, and Jawed Karim—created the service in February 2005. Google bought the site in November 2006 for US$1.65 billion; YouTube now operates as one of Google's subsidiaries.

YouTube allows users to upload, view, rate, share, add to favorites, report, comment on videos, and subscribe to other users. It offers a wide variety of user-generated and corporate media videos. Available content includes video clips, TV show clips, music videos, short and documentary films, audio recordings, movie trailers, live streams, and other content such as video blogging, short original videos, and educational videos. Most of the content on YouTube is uploaded by individuals, but media corporations including CBS, the BBC, Vevo, and Hulu offer some of their material via YouTube as part of the YouTube partnership program. Unregistered users can only watch videos on the site, while registered users are permitted to upload an unlimited number of videos and add comments to videos. Videos deemed potentially inappropriate are available only to registered users affirming themselves to be at least 18 years old.

YouTube earns advertising revenue from Google AdSense, a program which targets ads according to site content and audience. The vast majority of its videos are free to view, but there are exceptions, including subscription-based premium channels, film rentals, as well as YouTube Premium, a subscription service offering ad-free access to the website and access to exclusive content made in partnership with existing users.

As of February 2017, there were more than 400 hours of content uploaded to YouTube each minute, and one billion hours of content being watched on YouTube every day. As of August 2018, the website is ranked as the second-most popular site in the world, according to Alexa Internet.

Things have changed since YouTube was first invented. There has been a serious crackdown on suppressing videos and actually deleting accounts. Yes, we still have Freedom of Speech, but we do not own social media. These tools are owned and regulated. Be free with what you post but also be careful of what you post. You want to have the platform to promote your business, product or service but if you get shut down, it would not benefit you.

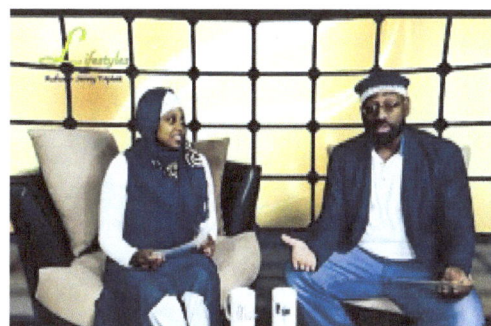

Surviving Marriage Webcast

People you should follow on YouTube:

His & Her Money

Will Smith

Roberto Blake

ET The Hip Hop Preacher

The North Star News

Jobs For Felons II: What Entrepreneurs Need To Know

Email Marketing

Depending on how long you have been in the prison system, you may have learned a little bit about email lists. You can build and expound on those lists with email marketing services and campaigns. You don't have to have hundreds of thousands of subscribers, but if you have a loyal following that supports you and shares your information, that is just as good.

Email marketing is still the most direct and effective way of connecting with your leads, nurturing them, and turning them into customers.

What Is Email Marketing?

Email marketing is the highly effective digital marketing strategy of sending emails to prospects and customers. Effective marketing emails convert prospects into customers, and turn one-time buyers into loyal, raving fans.

The Importance of Email Marketing

Despite the rise of social media and unsolicited spam (which is never a good marketing strategy, by the way), email remains the most effective way to nurture leads and turn them into customers.

Although there are many reasons you should make email marketing one of your top priorities, here are the 3 main ones...

1. Email is the #1 communication channel. Did you know that at least 91% of consumers check their email on a daily basis? That can't be said of any other communication channel.

2. You own your list. On any social media platform, your account (with all your fans) could be suspended or deleted at any time, for any reason, without notice. However, you own your email list. No one can take those leads away from you.

3. Email converts better. People who buy products marketed through email spend 138% more than those who do not receive email offers. In fact, email marketing has an ROI of 3800%. That's huge! And if you are wondering if social media converts even better, think again: the average order value of an email is at least three times higher than that of social media.

Email is simply the best way to make sales online.

Five Email Marketing Companies

1. MailChimp
2. Constant Contact
3. Aweber
4. Get Response
5. InfusionSoft

Jobs For Felons II: What Entrepreneurs Need To Know

To Blog or Not To Blog

To Blog or not to Blog, that is the question. If you are familiar with marketing channels, blogging is a huge one. You can write your story or the story of others or the story about your business, product or service and it can resonate with thousands of people. You can join a blog network and connect with like minded bloggers to help spread your message. A blog helps with you with three things:

1. A written story gets traction. You can self promote through storytelling
2. SEO – Search Engine Optimization. A blog will get ranked in google and help you become a subject matter expert
3. A blog can repurposed. You can turn a blog into a book, a video or a social media post. All of which will help you with bringing awareness to your book, business or product. And all for free.

There's a sweet spot when writing a blog. You want to keep it between 500 and 750 words. If you are writing with links and video, you can go a maximum of 1000 words to help get better rankings in Google. Either way, you can't go wrong with blogging. You don't even have to be a professional writer but you do have to know how to spell and tell a story.

Free Blogging Platforms
www.medium.com
www.patreon.com
www.blogger.com
www.buzzfeed.com
www.wordpress.com

Marketing

I'm not talking about old-school marketing communications. Companies are looking for expert online marketers who know how to create a buzz of inbound marketing or viral traffic through the web, social media, and content discovery. Writing a good press release just doesn't cut it anymore, as everyone is looking for the savvy online marketing professional who understands how the current state of the web operates and knows how to make it work to their benefit.

Analytics

Since data is becoming more and more accessible, smart companies are increasingly making decisions driven by metrics. Analytics is becoming a central hub across companies where everything (web, marketing, sales, operations) is being measured and each decision is supported by data. Thus, we are seeing a high level of demand for analytics and business intelligence professionals who almost act like internal consultants; they help determine what should be measured and then build out the capability for a

13

How To Write A Book In Less Than 90 Days

This Lesson was originally formatted as a webinar. Webinars are a great way of creating passive income.

How to Write a Book in Less Than 90 Days!

We always tell –people that everyone has a story to tell which means you at least have one book inside of you trying to get out. For some, it's a number of books or a series of books that should be written and on the book shelves. But before that time, you have to get the stories out of your head and on paper. That's not an easy chore if you don't consider yourself a wordsmith or even a great storyteller. No worries, we got you! Look for tips on the next page to get you started.

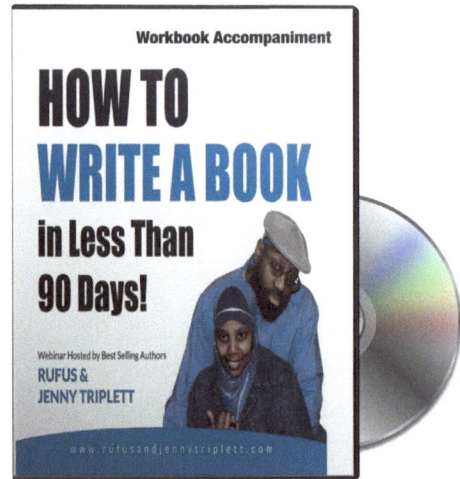

A webinar can be turned into a CD or DVD

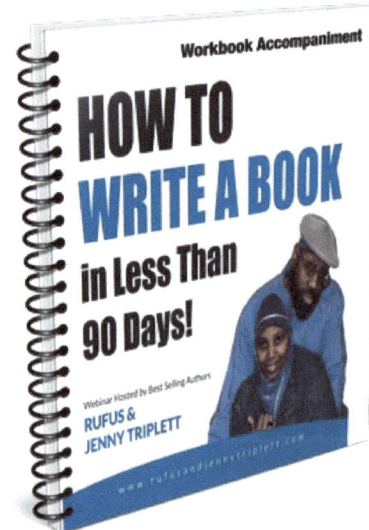

Get the CD & workbook here>>>
www.survivingbusinesstips.com

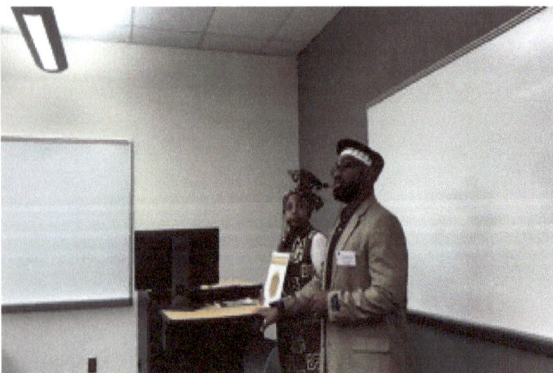

Happy Writing!

With the printing of this book, we have five titles in print with another going to print next year. We have sold over 100,000 books. They all started with an idea. Then we had to put in the work. You have to do the same. The only thing stopping you at this point…is you.

14

How to Outline a Book

•Get the thoughts out of your head

•What format should it be

•Should I write it, type it or record it

•Should I have a co-author or several co-authors or a ghost writer

•How should it start

How to come up with the Title of a Book

You don't have to start with the title

•The title may come from the book

•Make it short but catchy

•Don't make it too personal or unclear

•Does it make someone want to read it

How to Put Aside Time to Write a Book

In hour in the morning – an hour in the evening

• Put aside distractions

• Commit to the project

• Follow the outline

• Think about what you want to write during the day before you write it

• **How to know if your book is complete**

• Does it have a beginning, middle and end?

• Does it tell a relevant story?

• Does it give enough information and not leave several unanswered questions?

• If it is self-help, does it actually provide solutions?

• Does it flow?

How to decide if it's good enough or to rewrite?

• Let a few people read it
• Done is better than perfect
• Seek an editor for specific needs
• Could you read it over and over again without stumbling through it
• Did you miss a part of the story or give half information

15

How To Market A Book For Free

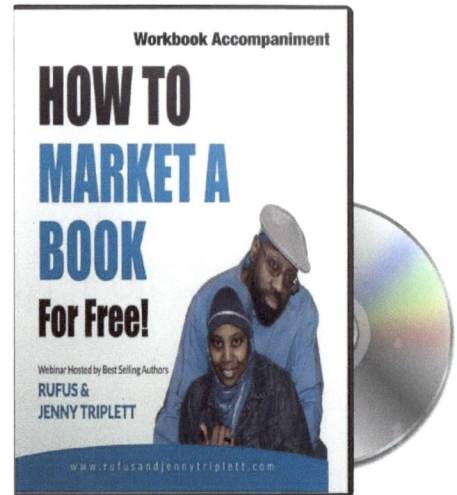

Webinars are a great way of creating passive income.

Marketing, Marketing Marketing!

It's a must. You must be marketing 85% of the time. You can have a great business, product or service but if no one knows about it, who is buying anything? There are several types of marketing and most do not learn the most of how it benefits and which type benefits you in school. Check out the next page for some cool marketing tips that you can do for FREE.

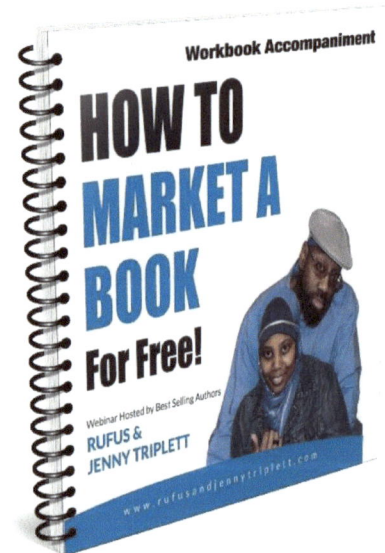

Marketing our business with Daymond John

We were fortunate to be VIP Ambassadors for Daymond John and with that personal signature boost form a Shark Tank alum it proved to be great marketing for our business.

One of the great promises of something being free is the skepticism that surrounds it…is it really free? Yes, most if the tips we give are absolutely free and you can use them to help you market but even if you give up an email address, it's still worth the give. Valuable information for the cost of a free email address is a no brainer. Even swap aint no swindle. And if it catapults your book to the Best Seller's List then that's the icing on the cake!

Obvious Free Marketing
- Don't be annoying by over self-promoting yourself on social media
- Guest Post on other Blogs
- Start Your Own Blog
- Start a YouTube channel
- Press Release

Ways to Market Your Book for Free
- Provide something for free to plug your own product
- Make graphics of excerpts of your book
- Post reviews frequently
- Ask someone to mention it on their video or blog
- Post links to your book page, website or Amazon page on blogs

Get more free marketing tips and information in the complete Set of How to Market a Book for Free

www.survivingbusinesstips.com

The Art of the 30 Second Pitch

A webinar can be turned into a CD or DVD

Webinars are a great way of creating passive income.

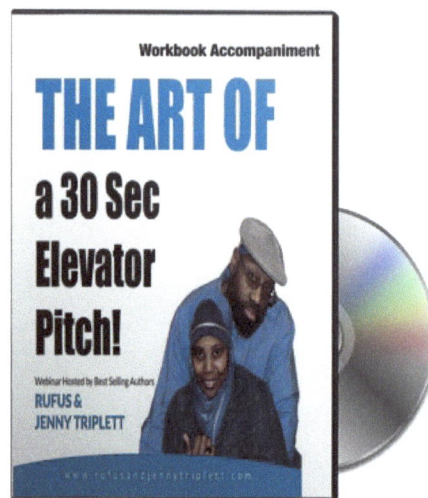

THE ELEVATOR PITCH

If you're not familiar with it, you might be asking yourself, what is it? If you have a business, product or service, then you should have an elevator pitch. Everyone is busy these days. Very busy. If you ever so happen stance to run across someone that gives you a few minutes of their time in order to pitch your business, you should be ready with a 30 second pitch. Find out on the next page some tips to make your pitch awesome!

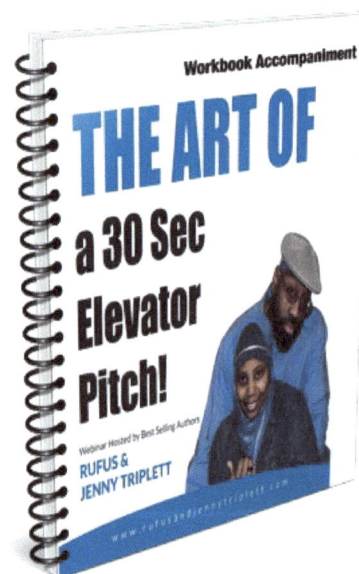

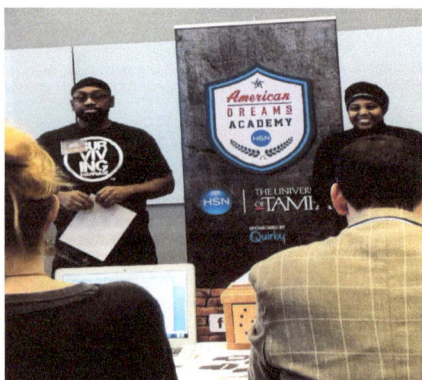

Pitching to HSN

Once the opportunities arises it's lights, camera action and it's a go. Be memorable. Be informative and have fun. The worst they can say is no.

Jobs For Felons II: What Entrepreneurs Need To Know

The great thing about being in business is knowing that you will one day have to describe that business to someone. Your passion may cause you to be long in your description when time does not ultimately allow for long windedness.

Sometimes life positions us to be in the company of influential people, if even by happen stance, and it's at these moments that you have to be prepared to pitch yourself, your product, your business, in the most effective manner in the least amount of time. It's always better to be prepared then to find out later you were not. Happy Pitching!

How to Compose a Pitch
- **Your Pitch should be full of authenticity, Passion & Purpose**
- **Stay away from clichés**
- **Shock factor is sometimes good but don't be gimmicky**
- **Why do you do what you do?**
- **(K) Keep (I) It (S) Simple (S) Samantha – simple talk. NO SAT words. NO science talk. NO exaggerating.**

Get more pitching tips and information in the complete Set of The Art of the 30 Second Elevator Pitch.

www.survivingbusinesstips.com

How To Speak For a Living

Before we go into this long spiel about how to parlay your book into speaking gigs, please note that every writer isn't a speaker and every speaker isn't a writer.

Sometimes what you write should stay on paper. Everyone can't articulate information and come across to an audience the way that they should in order to turn speaking into a living.

Now, with that said, let's talk about how you do that. The first thing you must do is commit. Commit to being a speaker and presenter. There are many ways that you can speak and make a living. You have to decide what you want to do. We educated you about social media because the doors are open for numerous opportunities if you use the tools available to you. Commit to learning how and what to do.

Start small. Start someplace local so you can get the nerves out. No matter how much you practice in front of the mirror, it doesn't mean that you will come across well or nail what you have to say. Depending on your content, see if a local boys or girls club will allow you to come speak. Kids are very receptive but they can also be your best and worst critics. Do a few local gigs like that to decide if this is really the path you want to take. If you like it and if it connects, then step up your game.

You can find speaking opportunities on Twitter and LinkedIn. If you scroll social media events, you can always pitch yourself as a speaker. It's not going to be easy but if you are persistent you can get a couple of gigs a month.

Never negate speaking for free. If it's something that works for you and you can network further opportunities out of it, go for it. For example, if you get the opportunity to be on stage with Mark Cuban, billionaire, owner of the Dallas Mavericks and resident shark of Shark Tank, but they aren't paying you anything, why would you turn that down? The exposure alone pays for itself. Put your best talk together and get prepared to shine. That would be something to have on your resume to leverage for other speaking gigs.

Don't be boring. Nobody likes a boring speaker. Even if you have a wealth of scientific information to present, try to do it in a way that captures the audience attention. Most boring speakers don't get asked back but if you do it fun and different, you'll be on the call back list year after year.

Always have a product to offer at the end. Most big platforms don't allow any selling from the stage but if you tell your story correctly or frame your presentation, people will be looking for you at the end to buy what you have to offer.

Jobs For Felons II: What Entrepreneurs Need To Know

Six Reasons Why Authors Should Participate in Book Fairs

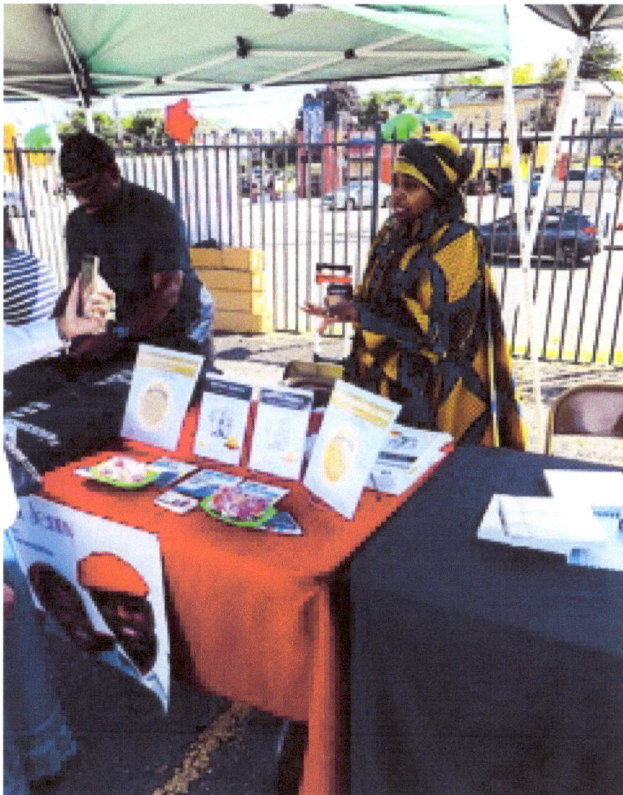

Soooo you've written a book. Great! Now how are you going to sell it? One of the greatest tools and outlets that authors have every year are book fairs. There are literally hundreds of them around the country that you can get involved and showcase your book(s). We have participated in several and here are six reasons why you should too:

Sell Books – The primary reason you go to a book fair is to sell books. That's it. It's the purpose for participation. Depending on when and where the book fair/festival is, you can actually sell hundreds of books. Some of the larger book fairs such as the Harlem Book Fair or The Book Expo in New York City, draws thousands of people and is totally focused on authors for book sales.

Awareness – Part of your marketing plan should include bringing awareness to your book and the fact that you are a published author and have a story to tell or an expertise to offer. Your marketing materials should include signage and a take away for the people that stop by your booth or table. We have found that the majority people that become aware of our books actually purchase our books.

Network with Community and Other Authors – There's nothing greater than being in the midst of Community. When you attend local book fairs, it brings you face to face with people that live and work in the community and allows you the opportunity to network with them for further opportunities. You also get to meet authors that you may or may not have heard of, hear their stories and connect for future endeavors.

Gain a Following – Book fairs allows you to the opportunity to increase your fan base. If you are relativity unknown or even somewhat a little known, you can list build with people signing up to stay in contact or with cool giveaways from your table/booth.

Media Attention – If the event is marketed and promoted well, you can get media attention from local or national news outlets for you and your book(s) Most news outlets are interested in covering things that help the community and you should also market via social media

Sell books – Yes, this was the first reason and the last reason why you should attend a book fair. Books are not meant to sit in the box they came in. Books are to be sold and distributed to the masses because you have a story to tell or you have something that will help someone else along the way. If the book fair/festival has time slots in which you can speak, be sure to try to get a spot on the schedule. Speaking and telling your story increases the likelihood that someone is going to buy your book.

Hope these tips are helpful. We have sold over 100,000 books and attending book fairs/festivals has given us a great boost. Being featured authors this year at Essencefest was not only great exposure but allowed our book to be elevated on the celebrity table.

We attended Philly's Iqra Book fair in September and as able to connect with numerous community people. Once you publish a book, it's up to you to continuously market it and promote it. You constantly have to keep reaching out to new eyes. People cannot buy a book if they don't know it exists. Have fun and happy traveling.

Jobs For Felons II: What Entrepreneurs Need To Know

NOTES

NOTES